THE
Old Photographs
SERIES
CHISWICK

Parish church of St Nicholas in the 1870s.

THE
Old Photographs
SERIES

CHISWICK

Compiled by
Carolyn & Peter Hammond

CHALFORD

BATH • AUGUSTA • RENNES

The country home of William Hogarth, the artist, between 1749 and 1764, seen in about 1902. At this time Hogarth Lane had not yet been widened into a trunk road and still had houses on either side.

Contents

Thames sailing barge alongside a wharf near Kew Bridge about 1906.

Introduction

Until the middle of the nineteenth century Chiswick was an area of market gardens and orchards with a population of about 6,000 people living in three small hamlets separated by open spaces: Strand on the Green along the riverside, Turnham Green along the High Road, the main road out of London to the west, and Old Chiswick around St Nicholas Church and along the Mall.

Local industries were influenced by the nearness of the river: fishing and boatbuilding are obvious examples but there were others such as brewing, malting, laundry work and soap and polish making which depended on water transport for deliveries of fuel and raw materials and in some cases the distribution of the finished products.

Because of its nearness to London, its pleasant surroundings and its reputation for being a healthy area Chiswick had early on become a fashionable and popular place to live. Many fine houses were built along the High Road and near the river. Among its well-known residents can be numbered the artists William Hogarth and Johann Zoffany, the writers Alexander Pope and W.B. Yeats and the architect C.F.A. Voysey.

By the end of the nineteenth century the area had been transformed, partly by the advent of public transport in the form of railways and the recently introduced trams and partly by the inexorable outward growth of London. It was now possible for more people to live in the pleasant outer suburbs such as Chiswick and travel to work in London daily. New roads were laid out on what had once been market gardens or the grounds of the large private houses. New shops, schools, churches and municipal services were provided and by the time of the 1901 census the population had increased to nearly 30,000.

In our choice of pictures we have tried to show both Chiswick's rural beginnings and how it changed in the twentieth century. Our major source for the illustrations was the Local History Collection at Chiswick Library, and we were fortunate that it included the work of several good professional photographers from the early years of this century such as F.H. Dann, Charles Henwood, H.R. Seymour and Wakefields, and also talented amateurs like the artist Nelson Dawson who lived on the Mall. The year 1994 marks the centenary of the birth of the picture postcard and we are very grateful to the postcard collectors (whose names are listed in the acknowledgements) who supplemented the Library's collection of postcards with many interesting examples from their own collections. Several firms were active in this area at the turn of the century such as R.J. Johns, the Photo Tourist Association of Heathfield Terrace and Wyndhams; their work includes both straightforward views of local streets, usually with a few interested spectators watching the photographer, and also evocative glimpses of special events like an early sale at Goodban's department store.

We have arranged the pictures in four sections covering respectively Old Chiswick, Grove Park, Strand on the Green and finally Turnham Green from the Hammersmith border to Chiswick Roundabout making detours down side turnings and taking in Bedford Park on the way.

We hope you enjoy looking at them as much as we enjoyed choosing them!

Acknowledgements

We acknowledge our indebtedness to those who have written on the history of Chiswick before us, and we wish to thank Valerie Bott and James Wisdom of the Brentford and Chiswick Local History Society, June Lewing of Gunnersbury Park Museum and Ruth Maranzi of Chiswick Library for their help in researching the captions to the photographs.

The majority of the photographs in this book have been taken from material in the collections at Chiswick Public Library and Gunnersbury Park Museum and we thank the London Borough of Hounslow Leisure Services Department for allowing us to use them. In some cases these were copied from originals held by other institutions or individuals and we would like to thank the following for permission to reproduce their photographs:

John Gillham: 60b, 61b & 128; Mrs and the late Mr J.W. Keating: 19; Mirror Syndication International: 95a; J.C. Newton: 111b; Mrs John Perkins: 105; Miss Eileen Richnell: 73a & 74b; Arthur Sanderson and Sons Ltd: 98 & 99; 1st Chiswick Scout Group: 79 & 121b, and Vosper Thornycroft (UK) Ltd: 24 & 25b.

We are most grateful to the following for allowing us to use material from their collections of postcards: Mrs Mary Brown: 40b, 41a & 96; Peter Downes: 43a, 44, 45a, 68b, 70a, 71a, 73b, 74a, 85b, 88b, 89b, 103b, 111a & 121a; S.J. Hayden of 7 Litchfield Avenue, Morden, Surrey, SM4 5QS: 30a, 91a, 93 & 126b, and P.J. Loobey of 231 Mitcham Lane, Streatham, London, SW16 6PY: 20a, 28b, 101a & 118a. The latter two have extensive collections of the original glass negatives of postcards printed by R.J. Johns.

One
Old Chiswick

The original village of Chiswick grew up around the church and the river crossing. It was a place of contrasts: from the Palladian splendour of Chiswick House to the fishermen's cottages of 'Sluts' Hole' with the fine houses along the Mall somewhere in between. Until the twentieth century it also contained most of the large scale industry of the area: two breweries, shipbuilding, and Chiswick Products' factory complex. It remained the administrative centre of the area until the 1870s despite the fact that even in 1801 Turnham Green had a bigger population than Old Chiswick.

Chiswick as it was seen from the river in the first half of the nineteenth century. A print of 1807 drawn by Schnebbelie.

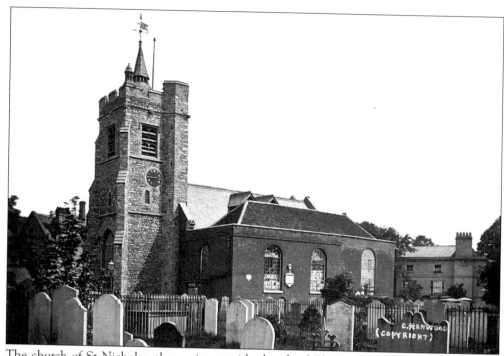

The church of St Nicholas, the ancient parish church of Chiswick, in the 1870s. The tower dates from the early fifteenth century, the north and south aisles from 1816 and 1777 respectively. The tower was retained when the church was rebuilt in 1882-84.

The interior of St Nicholas before rebuilding, showing the old box pews and galleries.

A view of the rebuilt St Nicholas church seen over the top of the cottages in Fisherman's Place in the 1930s. The cost of rebuilding the church, apart from a donation of £1000 from the Duke of Devonshire, was borne by Henry Smith of the Griffin Brewery.

The National School Room in the churchyard, next to the cottages in Fisherman's Place. A charity school was founded in the churchyard in 1706 and later became a National School; by the middle of the nineteenth century there were National Schools at Turnham Green and Strand as well. This building was demolished in 1951.

Looking down Church Street towards the river at the turn of the century. On the right is the church of St Nicholas, on the left is the Old Burlington, said to be the oldest house in Chiswick, which was a public house until 1924. This is one of the few remaining timber framed buildings left in Chiswick, from the period when brick and stone buildings were rare. On the extreme left can be seen the inn sign for the Lamb Tap, another public house served by the Lamb Brewery.

Opposite: Cottages in Fisherman's Place, which was previously known as Sluts' Hole. These old cottages were pulled down in the 1930s.

Walpole House in the 1930s. This is a late sixteenth century house refronted about 1730; said to be the last residence of Barbara Villiers, Duchess of Cleveland, mistress of Charles II. Thackeray was a pupil here when it was a school for young gentlemen and he may have used it as a model for Becky Sharp's School, Miss Pinkerton's Academy, in his *Vanity Fair*.

The back view of College House, the home of the Chiswick Press from 1816 until 1852. The figure in the garden is probably one of the daughters of Charles Whittingham the younger, owner of the Press. Whittingham's sons were apprenticed to the business and his daughters designed decorative borders for the books. The house stood on the eastern corner of the Mall and Chiswick Lane until it was demolished in 1875 and Heron, Staithe and Suffolk Houses plus Thames Bank built in its place. It had replaced the prebendal Manor house which was originally used for boys of Westminster School in times of sickness in London. The original of this photograph appears to have been printed from a paper negative, a photographic technique common in the 1840s and it may thus be the oldest surviving photograph of Chiswick.

Mawson's Row before 1914 when the Maynard family held the licence of the Mawson Arms and the Fox and Hounds. This double name came about when the Fox and Hounds closed and the Mawson Arms, which was very near, took over the licence. Mawson's Row itself was built in the early eighteenth century by Thomas Mawson, who owned the Griffin Brewery, now Fuller, Smith and Turner. Before it became the Mawson Arms the corner house was occupied in 1716-19 by the poet Alexander Pope and his parents.

Title page of a book published by the Chiswick Press.

THE

ESSAY ON MAN,

AND

OTHER POEMS.

BY

ALEXANDER POPE.

CHISWICK:
From the Press of C. Whittingham,
COLLEGE HOUSE.
SOLD BY R. JENNINGS, POULTRY; T. TEGG, CHEAPSIDE;
A. K. NEWMAN AND CO. LEADENHALL STREET; LONDON:
J. SUTHERLAND, EDINBURGH;
AND RICHARD GRIFFIN AND CO. GLASGOW.

1822.

The first wireless set for use by patients was installed at Chiswick Hospital in 1926. The hospital was built towards the eastern end of the Mall in 1912 by Dan Mason, founder of Chiswick Products, as a Cottage Hospital for the people of Chiswick. It was rebuilt in 1936, later became a maternity hospital and is now an old people's home.

Christmas in the children's ward of Chiswick Hospital in 1927.

A group of brewery workers from the Griffin brewery of Fuller, Smith and Turner at the turn of the century, each carrying the tools of their trade. The prosperous-looking man in the centre may be the Master Brewer. The origins of this brewery go back to the seventeenth century.

Osier cutters on Chiswick Eyot in the mid-1920s. The osiers were made into baskets for the market gardeners of the area to transport their produce and into eel and fish traps. The cutters have waited until high tide to float their load to the bank and thus avoid the need to carry it across the mud.

Bill Fishlock, who had been a ferryman at Chiswick, and his wife Annie in his ferryboat *Dorothy* in 1928. The ferry ran from the foot of Church Street to the Barnes bank, from at least the seventeenth century until the 1930s.

A traditional Thames wherry in about 1925 just leaving the Chiswick bank, the photographer is probably standing on the causeway at the foot of Church Street. A photograph belonging to Bill Fishlock's family.

Unloading barges at high tide directly into carts at Chiswick Eyot, near the draw dock, photographed in the 1920s.

The Boat Race in 1890 with the Oxford and Cambridge crews and their following boats (including river tugs) passing Chiswick Steps. Oxford won by a bare length after a hard fought race. The enormous crowds on both banks are very noticeable. The Boat Race regularly attracted huge crowds; this was probably Chiswick's busiest day of the year.

Men unloading coal barges at the draw dock near the bottom of Chiswick Lane about 1905. The draw dock was a gently sloping bank at which keel-less boats, such as Thames sailing barges, could be safely unloaded. A photograph by Nelson Dawson, an artist, silversmith and photographer resident on Chiswick Mall from 1897 until his death in 1941.

The sewage works off Corney Road under construction in 1878. The Improvement Commissioners (the predecessors of the Local Board, see below) and their staff are here inspecting the work. William Trehearne the Surveyor can be seen with his theodolite.

A peaceful scene on Chiswick Mall in the 1880s, immediately opposite the site of College House. The cart belongs to the Chiswick Local Board, which was responsible for running local services before the Urban District Council was set up in 1894.

A group of the men involved in building the Corney Road Sewage works posing in front of their stationary steam engine with the Commissioners at the back. This major work of the Improvement Commissioners was to provide main drainage for the rapidly developing area and prevent sewage being discharged directly into the Thames.

The launch of the HMS *Speedy*, torpedo gunboat, from the Church Wharf yards of Messrs Thornycroft in May 1893. The company started building boats in Chiswick in the 1860s and built over 400 including launches, torpedo gunboats and destroyers. As the boats got bigger it became more and more difficult to get them down the Thames and under the bridges to the open sea, the first bridge at Hammersmith being particularly low. They were therefore compelled to start transferring their boat building works to Southampton in 1904.

One of the last torpedo boats built at Chiswick.

A Thornycroft steam lorry; the firm diversified into building cars and lorries after 1896.

A splendid steam roller on Chiswick Mall in about 1908, presumably from the Chiswick Urban District Council fleet, photographed by Nelson Dawson.

Church Street about 1905, looking towards the Old Burlington and the river. The house on the extreme left was the home of Arthur Sich, a partner in the Lamb Brewery, which was situated behind the houses on the left.

A view of the top of Church street about 1906 at the junction of Devonshire Road and Burlington Lane. When Burlington Lane was widened in the 1930s to become the Great Chertsey Road the buildings on the left were destroyed.

Boston House in Chiswick Square photographed early this century. The house was a school in the early 19th century (possibly that described by Thackeray in *Vanity Fair* - but see also page 14) and later a convent. In 1922 it was bought by Chiswick Products as a social centre for their staff. It has now been converted back to housing. It is said to be haunted by the ghost of a Lady Boston, murdered by her husband.

Chiswick Memorial Homes in Burlington Lane, built with money raised locally as a memorial to the dead of the Great War. They were opened in July 1922 to provide homes for disabled servicemen.

One of the entrances to Chiswick Products in Burlington Lane in the 1930s. It was founded by the Mason family in the 1870s as the Chiswick Soap Company and was later known as the Chiswick Polish Company; Cherry Blossom boot polish and Mansion floor polish were two products that became household names. It was absorbed by Reckitt and Colman in 1954 and production was moved to Hull in 1972.

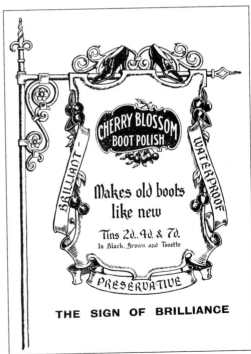

CHERRY BLOSSOM
BOOT POLISH

BRILLIANT

WATERPROOF

Makes old boots
like new

Tins 2d., 4d. & 7d.
In Black, Brown and Tonette

PRESERVATIVE

THE SIGN OF BRILLIANCE

An advertisement for one of Chiswick Products' best known polishes.

Burlington Lane in the 1920s looking towards the junction with Hogarth Lane, now the Hogarth Roundabout. On the right is the entrance to St Mary's Convent and St Joseph's Hospital.

The entrance to St Joseph's Hospital about the mid-1920s. The Anglican Sisters of the Order of St Mary and St John came to Chiswick in the 1890s and built their hospital for the handicapped with the advice of Florence Nightingale. They amalgamated with the Order of St Margaret in 1910.

Hogarth Lane, looking west towards Hogarth House in the 1920s. Since the 1950s this has become a busy trunk road, the A4.

The country house of William Hogarth, painter and engraver, seen from Hogarth Lane before the First World War. Hogarth occupied it as his summer residence from 1749 until his death in 1764. By the late nineteenth century it had fallen into disrepair and was bought and restored by Colonel Shipway of Grove House and opened to the public in 1902. Col. Shipway gave the house to the Middlesex County Council in 1909 for use as a Hogarth museum; admission then cost 6d.

A cycling club outing in the early 1890s, photographed outside the gates of Chiswick House, at the bottom of Duke's Avenue. Cycling was a very popular hobby and there were at least three cycling clubs in the area at that time. The Duke of Devonshire had purchased the gates in 1837, they were moved to Devonshire House in Piccadilly in 1897 and are now at the entrance to Green Park in Piccadilly.

Opposite: The opening of Chiswick House grounds to the public by HRH Prince George, later Duke of Kent, in 1929. The estate had been bought by the Middlesex County Council in 1929, with the help of contributions from George V and the Chiswick Urban District Council amongst others. It was then leased to the UDC for use as a public park.

Chiswick House photographed before 1952 when the wings were demolished, showing the north and south wings designed for the fifth Duke of Devonshire. These replaced the old Jacobean mansion and were planned to transform the house into a suitable country seat and were added c.1788-93.

The stable block of the original Jacobean Chiswick House being demolished in 1933. The seventeenth century house itself had been demolished in 1788 to make way for the building of the wings to Lord Burlington's Palladian villa.

Two

Grove Park

Grove Park was the last major area of Chiswick to be developed as much of it was part of large private estates which were not broken up until the latter part of the 19th century. However with the coming of the railways there was an increasing demand for housing in the area. The builders of the new estates emphasised the spacious layout amidst pleasant rural surroundings, the nearness of the river and the good social and sporting facilities of the area.

A detail from a developer's map of 1867 giving an idealistic view of how the estate would appear once it was built.

Grove House, in the 1920s. This was a Tudor house remodelled in the eighteenth century. It was owned by the Chiswick benefactor Col. Shipway from 1895 and was demolished in 1928 after his death. Kinnaird Avenue was built on its site. Grove House was one of the few large houses in Chiswick which remained a private home for the whole of its life from the early 1530s when it was built until it was demolished.

The Drawing Room of Grove House when owned by Col. Shipway. The Colonel was apparently fond of hunting.

The Sitting Room of Grove House when owned by Col. Shipway.

Cubitt's yacht basin in the 1920s. It was originally a lake in Grove House grounds. During the First World War a lock was constructed and the basin used to manufacture concrete barges; here it is being used as the home of a motor yacht club, later it was used for mooring houseboats. The site is now occupied by the marina and luxury housing of Chiswick Quay.

In 1923 Chiswick UDC bought nearly 200 acres of riverside land from the Duke of Devonshire; by 1926 they had laid it out as a recreational area with a terraced river side walk, a bandstand, shelters and sports pitches.

Swimmers enjoying a fine day at Chiswick Open Air Baths in June 1931. These baths, opened in 1910 in Edensor Road, were one of the first open air baths in London. At first the sexes were strictly segregated except at weekends when family bathing was allowed, but the rules had been relaxed by the 1930s.

Part of Grove Park Farm, owned by the Jessop family, taken from Burlington Lane in 1908. Chiswick School now occupies the site of the farmhouse.

Chiswick County School for Girls, opened in 1916. Chiswick County School for Boys opened on an adjacent site in 1926. The two schools were amalgamated to form a co-educational grammar school in 1966 and became part of a comprehensive in 1968 with Staveley Road School.

The fifth form of Chiswick County School for Girls in 1921.

The English room of Staveley Road Boys School in the 1930s.

Sutton Court just before it was demolished in the early 1900s. Sutton Court was one of the two manors of Chiswick. This house was probably built in the late eighteenth century and later became a boarding school for boys, kept by Frederick Tappenden from 1845 until he died in 1879. In the 1880s the house was occupied by W.J. Compton, the Chairman of the Local Board. An earlier house on the site was lived in by Lady Fauconberg, Oliver Cromwell's daughter. The window of the stables, seen on the right, was transferred to the Clifton Works in Grove Park Terrace, headquarters of Richard Arundell, the builder who developed much of Grove Park.

Sutton Court Mansions: the first block of flats on the site of Sutton Court was built in 1904.

The dining room of one of the flats in Sutton Court Mansions in 1910.

Home for Motherless Girls, The Roystons, Grove Park, Chiswick.

The Roystons was built in the 1870s on the corner of Bolton and Spencer Roads. In May 1900 Mr R T Smith, founder of the Chiswick Mission, opened a Home here for Motherless Girls whose fathers could not look after them. There was a similar home for boys in Burlington Lane. The building has now been converted to flats.

A Group of Motherless Girls from The Roystons,

Residents of the Roystons Home for Motherless Girls, taken about 1910.

Grove Park Hotel in the early 1900s, one of the first buildings to be completed in the developing Grove Park estate, a focus for the sports and social life of the area.

Level crossing in Grove Park Terrace, about 1910. Originally there was a second level crossing near the Grove Park Hotel, but this was replaced by the road bridge over the railway built in 1897–8.

In the 1930s a new route was opened up from Chiswick to Richmond involving a new bridge over the Thames. This photograph is looking from the Chiswick bank.

Chiswick Bridge nearing completion. It was opened in July 1933 by HRH the Prince of Wales.

Three
Strand on the Green

In 1706 it was described as 'a straggling place inhabited chiefly by fishermen'. Other river related industries grew up there as well: boat building and repair, malting and laundering which both relied on the river as a cheap means of transporting raw materials. When members of the royal family started living at Kew in the 18th century the surrounding areas also became fashionable and bigger houses appeared among the small cottages. Then as the industries declined so the area has become almost entirely residential and much sought after for its picturesque appearance.

A panorama of the western part of Strand taken in 1923. Boat building and repair yards and the kiln roofs of malt houses can be seen. In the distance is the third Kew Bridge, opened in 1903 by Edward VII.

Old cottages, before the First World War. One hundred years ago many of the people living on Strand would have been employed in the local industries and living in such cottages as these.

Fine eighteenth century houses on Strand, shown at high tide. Houses such as these were built especially after the opening of the first Kew Bridge in 1759, which improved transport links and made Strand more popular as a residential area.

Opposite: The City Barge Public House (originally the Maypole) in the late 1920s, so named in honour of the City of London state barge. This was kept in a barge house on the opposite bank when it was no longer required for ceremonial purposes. The City Barge was badly damaged by a land mine in 1940 and the only part remaining of the original building is the old Bar below the level of the footpath.

The original Bell and Crown Public House in the early 1900s, a building dating back to the eighteenth century. It was demolished in 1907 to make way for the present Bell and Crown. Public houses were used as places for recreation and for the transaction of business; the steps in front were to help passengers boarding boats, the equivalent of the modern bus stop.

Kew railway bridge early this century. It was built in 1868 to carry the London and South Western Railway (now the District Line) to Richmond. Charles Murrell, barge builders, situated next to the City Barge 1902-27 can be seen on the left. On the bridge can be seen one of the steam trains of the L&SW Railway.

Residents outside the Alms Houses, c.1910. These were six single room alms houses built in 1724 on the site of a seventeenth century poor house. They were renovated in 1933 by County Councillor Hopkin Morris and modernised in 1974.

Another view of the Alms Houses, next to the splendidly named British Buffalo Marine Motor Company.

Dr Stella Churchill (prospective Labour Party candidate for Brentford and Chiswick) opening the Infant Welfare Centre in May 1928 in St Paul's Church Institute in Pyrmont Road. This was run by a committee of local residents with Dr Churchill as the honorary medical officer.

Bommer Pearce, one of the last commercial fishermen on the Thames, in 1895. Pearce is shown here with his 'Peter boat' (a double ended fishing boat) drawn up on the shore just west of the Bell and Crown.

Eel boats were a common sight on the river until the 1890s. This is a 'Peter boat', here used as an eel boat, the fisherman is baiting eel pots.

Kew Bridge and the Pier House Laundry at the end of the nineteenth century. The Laundry was established in 1860 and expanded into new buildings north of the road in 1905. The bridge is the second one on this site and was built in 1789 to replace the original wooden bridge.

The Pier House Laundry in about 1900. Here delicate fabrics are being washed by hand.

A malthouse in use in the 1890s, demolished in 1925. The tall conical kiln was used for roasting the grain after germination.

Smoking break on the waterfront in the 1920s.

High tide, spring 1937 - the hazards of living by the river and the reason for the steps up to the doorways of so many Strand houses. The Greater London Council funded major flood defences in the mid-1970s.

Four

Turnham Green

Turnham Green grew up as the result of the traffic along the main road leading from London to the west. Originally the name covered all the area from the Hammersmith boundary to Gunnersbury. Because of its nearness to London and its reputation as a healthy spot it had become a fashionable area to live by the end of the 17th century, with large houses lining the High Road as well as numerous inns to serve the travellers. Later many of the large houses were turned into schools or other institutions and eventually demolished to be replaced by streets of terraced housing which often bear the name of the estate they replaced. As the population increased towards the end of the 19th century Turnham Green became more important than Old Chiswick with the municipal buildings such as the Town Hall, the Fire Station, the Library, the Police Station and the main shopping area all sited in or near the High Road.

Chiswick Town Hall on the south side of Turnham Green as it appeared after the extensive enlargements carried out in 1901; the core of the building remains the original Vestry Hall built for conducting parish business in 1875. The Crown in the pediment is probably part of decorations for the coronation of George V in 1911.

Young's Corner, a painting of about 1880. This was the traditional boundary of Hammersmith with Chiswick, so-called from Charles Young's grocery and post office. The wooden building on the left was part of a thirteen acre market garden.

Young's Corner about ten years later. By then Young's shop had closed.

Young's Corner early this century. It was rebuilt in 1894 and the electric tram service was started in 1901.

Horse tram at Young's Corner, between 1894 and 1901. From 1882 horse trams ran to and from Shepherds Bush down Goldhawk Road and connected with a service along the High Road to Kew Bridge.

Hammersmith and Chiswick Station in 1958. This stood on the north side of Chiswick High Road near Young's Corner and was built by the North and South Western Junction Railway. A passenger service was started in 1858 but withdrawn in 1916 due to lack of demand. The goods service continued until 1965, mainly for coal.

The deserted platform of the Hammersmith and Chiswick Station in 1933, looking south towards the High Road. The Ravensmede Estate was built on the site in 1977.

A 1965 view of the Bath Road level crossing on the North and South Western Junction Railway, looking north. In an effort to encourage local traffic three halts were opened in 1909, including one at Bath Road, but they were all closed in 1916 when the passenger service was withdrawn.

The central power house built on the north side of the High Road just west of Merton Avenue by London United Tramways to provide power for the electric trams which started to run along the High Road in 1901. The Power House has now been converted into flats and studios.

The machine shop for servicing the electric trams of the London United Tramways.

Elaborate iron work and switch gear in the engine room in the power house in 1901. This Switch Board, on an ornamental gallery nine feet above the floor, was divided into two parts, one half for 'continuous-current panels' and the other for 'three-phase panels'. It controlled seven generators for the current, the largest of which generated 1000 kilowatts.

Annual allotment show for the children at Beverley Road School in September 1927. They are taking the fruit and vegetables to Chiswick Hospital. The School was opened in March 1926, having been built on the site of All Saints Mission Church. It closed in 1978.

The Roebuck on the High Road was one of the coaching inns which grew up to serve travellers on this busy road. The stables can be seen through the archway on the left. This view shows it in 1890 before it was pulled down in 1893 and replaced by shops and the present Roebuck on the same site.

Manor Farm House in the early 1880s. It was built on the west side of Chiswick Lane in the late seventeenth century by Sir Stephen Fox. In 1851 it became a lunatic asylum run by the Tuke family who introduced more enlightened ways of treating mental disorders. After the Tukes moved to larger premises at Chiswick House in 1896 the house was demolished. Wilton Avenue stands on the site of the garden and house.

A busy scene in Turnham Green Terrace, near the junction with the High Road, dating from about 1905 or just after, when the single storey shops were built on a filled in drainage ditch on the west side of the Terrace.

Turnham Green Terrace, near Turnham Green Station, in about 1900, before the railway line was widened to accommodate the Piccadilly Line in 1911.

Turnham Green Station in the early 1900s. It was opened in 1869 when the trains of the London and South Western Railway ran from Richmond to the City. In 1879 the line to Ealing was opened. On the extreme right can be seen the original steps leading to the platforms.

Turnham Green Station about 1912 seen from the north, with motor cabs lined up awaiting passengers.

Bath Road Corner showing the premises of Thomas Johnson, Nurseryman, who was at Bedford Park from about 1895 until the mid-1920s. He also had premises near Chiswick Park station and at the top of Sutton Court Road. This card was sent some time before 1908 by Johnson to a client, 'Hoping to receive your favours'.

Bedford Park

The area north of Turnham Green Station, known as Bedford Park, was developed in the 1870s to provide affordable housing for those of artistic aspirations but limited means. The houses were designed in a red brick 'Queen Anne' style in tree-lined roads, some from drawings by the well known architect Richard Norman Shaw. He also designed most of the public buildings. This chromolithograph of The Avenue, by J.C. Dollman, is one of a set of nine views of Bedford Park published in 1882, each one contributed by an artist resident in the area. The white fencing, a particular feature of the estate, may be seen.

Bath Road in about 1900, showing the church of St Michael and all Angels, the Stores and the Tabard Inn, all designed by Richard Norman Shaw and opened in 1880 to provide the centre of the self contained Bedford Park community.

St. Michael's Church, Bedford Park, W 0702.

St Michael and All Angels, Bedford Park in the 1900s. The many trees serve to illustrate that Bedford Park was living up to its reputation for being the precursor of the Garden City movement.

BATH ROAD, BEDFORD PARK.

The Chiswick School of Art in Bath Road in about 1904. It was designed by Maurice Adams, (an architect living in Bedford Park), and Richard Norman Shaw and opened in October 1881. It became the Chiswick and Acton Polytechnic in 1899 and the Chiswick Polytechnic in 1928 and then in 1944 the building was destroyed by a flying bomb. It was rebuilt about 1949 and eventually closed in July 1982, just after celebrating its hundredth anniversary.

One of the art rooms in the School of Art, from the prospectus of 1903-04. Classes in every form of drawing and painting were given, and by then also in various other subjects such as building trades, engineering and commercial studies.

Chiswick Ladies Hockey Club 1st eleven in 1896/97. The Club was founded in 1895 by the ladies of the Bedford Park Lawn Tennis Club and quickly became known in hockey circles for producing very good players. They originally played in yellow blouses with black ties and black serge skirts six inches off the ground - a special concession only allowed on condition that immediately a match was over they changed back into 'respectable' floor length skirts.

Cecil Aldin, one of the Bedford Park colony of artists, driving his donkey cart along Queen Anne's Gardens in 1898. Aldin kept a number of donkeys as well as other animals.

Bath Road in the 1920s after heavy rain (or a minor flood) had raised the wood blocks of which many main roads were constructed. Later when the roads were re-surfaced with tarmac the blocks were sold for fuel.

South Parade looking east from the corner of Esmond Road, a typical Bedford Park road, built in the early 1880s. This postcard was franked in 1908.

The dining room of a Bedford Park house about 1900, showing a pewter dining service popular at the turn of the century.

A path leading to Turnham Green Station in the 1920s across Back Common, south of the railway embankment and north of Back Common Road.

Back Common between Victor Villas and the railway, shortly after it was laid out for recreation in 1912.

Old cottages on Back Common, being demolished to make way for Victor Villas, which were completed in 1907.

The first Windmill Public House in the 1890s, on the corner of Windmill Road and the High Road.

The Windmill being demolished at the end of the nineteenth century to make way for a new public house. The building on the left is Rankins the drapers, with Windmill Alley leading to Back Common.

A view up Windmill Road towards Back Common, on the left the Windmill Public House which was rebuilt about 1900. In the distance can be seen the cottages which stood to the west of Castle Place, now a grassed over area. Note on the right the entrance to the yard of the old Police Station where the policemen kept their bicycles.

The front view of the late Victorian Windmill Public House from the High Road, photographed during a Scout procession in 1962, just before it was demolished in turn and replaced by the present building in 1964.

Annandale House on the south side of the High Road in the 1870s. The home of the Marquess of Annandale in the eighteenth century. It was demolished in 1880 and Annandale Road built on the site.

A room in Annandale House, possibly the Study, just before it was demolished when it was occupied by Dr William Leigh.

Queuing for water at a standpipe in Wood Street, off Devonshire Road, during bitterly cold weather in February 1929. The edges of the Thames had frozen and the Port of London Authority were running a special tug up and down the river to break up the ice floes and keep a navigation channel open. Wood Street and the neighbouring roads of early nineteenth century small houses were demolished after the Second World War.

Looking north up Devonshire Road from the corner of Hogarth Lane in the 1920s. On the right can be seen Chiswick Parish Church Hall, opened in February 1898. It was demolished in the 1950s to make way for the widening of the A4.

Number 183 in the High Road between the wars. A laundry collecting office was on this site from 1907, here it is acting for the Victoria House Laundry. This bow window still survives as part of a book shop. Laundries were a major industry in the area.

Chiswick Fire Station. W 5923

General view of the south side of the High Road between Devonshire Road and Linden Gardens in about 1910. It shows the Fire Station (opened in 1891), earlier versions of the public houses the Prince of Wales and the George IV, and some shops familiar until recently, such as Landgrebe's Bakery and Gerard's Ironmongers.

Fire Station, with firemen parading with their motorised equipment (which they obtained in 1910), just before the First World War. The tall tower was used to dry the leather hoses before rolling them up and to store the long escape ladder.

Firemen outside the Station in 1902, with the Station decorated for the coronation of Edward VII. The firemen were all volunteers who lived close to the Fire Station. In a busy year they would have attended nearly fifty calls, but as few as twenty-five in quieter years.

A horse drawn fire engine posing for a photograph about 1905.

Street market in the High Road outside the George IV public house, in the early 1920s. At that time the Gill family held the licence for the George IV and were also connected with other public houses in the area. The laundry shop with the bow window is here acting for the Atlas Laundry.

Opposite: Earl Jellicoe opening the British Legion Club in April 1926 in the second Linden House, now the site of the modern Police Station opened in 1972. On the left can be seen the curved roof of the new indoor market.

Indoor market opened in 1926 next door to Linden House to replace the outdoor street market. Business declined within a few years and the building was used by the fire service from 1937.

High Road frontage in 1878 of the original Linden House, one of the large houses built along the High Road in the 18th and 19th centuries. The residence of Thomas Griffiths Wainwright, a notorious 19th century murderer. The house was demolished in 1878 and Linden Gardens built on its site in 1882.

Linden Gardens before the First World War. The sender of this postcard has marked the house where he is staying with an 'X'.

The cinema called the Electric Theatre was opened on the corner of Duke Road and the High Road in 1911. It was later called the Coliseum, and when it closed in 1933 it was known as the Tatler. The building still exists converted into a row of three shops.

Hogarth School in the 1920s seen from the south end of Duke Road. It was opened in 1884 with girls in the building on the left, now St Mary's RC School, and boys on the right in what is now the Hogarth Youth Centre. In 1958 it was reorganised as a junior mixed school and moved into a new building in Devonshire Street next to Hogarth Infants' School.

Afton House in 1885. It is one of the few surviving examples of the large houses built along the High Road in the 18th century and is now the Chiswick Memorial Club. During its long history it has been a private house, a school and a laundry. In 1919 Dan Mason of Chiswick Products bought it and opened it as a centre for ex-servicemen. The front garden seen here has now been swallowed up by Bourne Place and the Times Furnishing building.

Clifton Gardens, looking north from the High Road towards the Postmen's Sorting Office in the 1920s. Most of the road was demolished in the mid-1970s to make way for the Health Centre and new housing.

The Postmen's Sorting Office in Clifton Gardens in 1972. It operated from the mid-1890s until 1967 when the sorting operations transferred to the new building in Heathfield Terrace.

A group of postmen outside the Sorting Office before the First World War, in the uniform (including the distinctive cap) worn during the first part of the century.

Chiswick postmen on the morning of 25th December 1925, sorting mail for delivery on Christmas Day.

The south side of the High Road showing the Catholic Church and the Times Furnishing store in the 1920s; notice how the building extended right to the corner of Duke's Avenue. The Post Office operated from the building on the right from the time of the First World War until it moved to new premises in Heathfield Terrace in 1967. The building is now used by the TSB.

The corner of Duke's Avenue and the High Road showing the temporary repairs to the damage caused by the bomb which fell on 19th February 1944, demolishing part of the Times Furnishing shop and damaging eight other shops and the church. Traffic in the High Road was stopped for over a week. In the background can be seen the North Lodge, known in 1851 as the Duke's Lodge, on the corner of Bourne Place and Duke's Avenue. It later served as a depot for Express Dairies until it was demolished in 1968. The Roman Catholic Parish Centre was opened in 1980 on the site.

The first V2 rocket of the Second World War fell outside number 5 Staveley Road on 8th September 1944 killing three people, damaging over 500 houses and leaving a 20 ft deep crater in the road.

Officials inspecting the crater in Staveley Road. The story was that the explosion was caused by a gas main bursting, an explanation not locally believed in view of the official interest. This was the only V2 rocket to fall in Chiswick.

The Public Library in about 1900. It first opened in 1890 in the house on the corner of Bourne Place and Duke Road but it soon outgrew these premises and the Sanderson family offered their house in Duke's Avenue. The Library moved into its new home in 1898 where it still is. This view shows the building soon after the Library moved in when it still looked like a private house.

The book issuing desk in the lending library in the 1940s showing how the tickets and book cards were filed in long wooden trays; no computers then.

The newspaper and magazine reading room in the extension added to the south side of the library building in 1931. This room is now the children's library.

Sanderson's new wallpaper factory building, erected in 1902-3 on the north side of Barley Mow Passage. The architect was C.F.A. Voysey, who had also designed wallpaper patterns for Sanderson's. This was the only industrial building he designed.

An early Sanderson advertisement.

Sanderson's wallpaper factory on the south side of Barley Mow Passage in about 1901. Arthur Sanderson had set up his factory on part of the site of the old militia barracks in 1879.

The Sanderson Wallpaper factory after the great fire in October 1928. On the right of the picture can be seen the Library building which was badly damaged in the fire and not reopened until 1931. The fire destroyed most of the factory but within three months temporary floors had been installed and production recommenced. A new factory was built in Perivale and all work was transferred there in 1929.

Mr Alfred Goodall, the caretaker at the Library since 1899 clearing up after the great fire of October 1928. The Library remained closed (although a temporary service was provided from huts in Belmont School grounds) while the building was renovated and a new wing built on to the south side, housing the reference library, junior library and the reading room. It reopened in March 1931.

Duke's Avenue looking towards the gates to Chiswick House. The road was first created in the 1820s by the 6th Duke of Devonshire to form an approach to Chiswick House from the High Road and did not become a public road until the 1880s.

The junction of Duke's Avenue, Park Road and Barrowgate Road in the 1930s. An early form of public telephone box can be seen in the centre of the picture. At that time it was possible to look right down Park Road before the A4 cut off its northern end.

The Royal Horticultural Society show grounds in 1851. In 1821 the Society leased 33 acres of land (roughly the area between Duke's Avenue and Sutton Court Road, south of Heathfield Terrace, and down to the A4) from the 6th Duke of Devonshire to set up its new display grounds. These were mainly for fruit and vegetables but also included an arboretum and ornamental plants. In 1870 the grounds were reduced in size to the south where Barrowgate Road was later developed. The Gardens finally moved to Wisley in 1903. The regular shows held by the Society brought large crowds to Chiswick. This lithograph of a fête shows on the extreme right the tower of Christ Church, Turnham Green, built in 1843.

The corner of the High Road and Heathfield Terrace just before the First World War, looking east towards the Roman Catholic church.

An early sale at Goodban's store, about 1910. Mr Percy Goodban took over the store in 1909 from William Soper (whose name can still be seen lettered on the facade), and sold it to Mr Cecil Cooper, who retained the name, in 1928. It closed in 1974 on the retirement of Cecil Cooper's son John. The building is now used by Boots and Robert Dyas.

Belmont House in the late nineteenth century. It stood on the north side of the High Road opposite the Barley Mow public house and was a boarding school at this time. It was demolished towards the end of the century to make way for shops. This school was one of many private boarding schools which flourished in the area in the eighteenth and nineteenth centuries. Is the imposing figure in the doorway the headmaster?

The Palais Cinema, Chiswick's first purpose built cinema, open from 1910 to 1914. It stood on the site of the present Woolworths in the High Road.

A festive occasion on Turnham Green in the mid-nineteenth century, including a cricket match. Cricket has been played on the Green since at least this time. The soldiers in uniform probably came from the militia barracks on the south side of Heathfield Terrace where the Army and Navy Stores later built their furniture depository.

A lithograph of Christ Church, the church on Turnham Green, made soon after it was built in 1843 to provide a more conveniently sited church than St Nicholas for the growing population in the north of the parish. The church was designed by George Gilbert Scott. This view shows the east end before the additions of 1887.

The interior of Christ Church before the chancel and north east chapel were added in 1887. The pews in the centre aisle were some of the free ones for poorer people; pew rents were payable on most of the others.

The procession from Christ Church passing the Town Hall on 24th October 1913 to lay the foundation stone (laid by the Bishop of Kensington) for the new Church Hall in Heathfield Gardens.

Procession of the Lord Lieutenant of Middlesex and the Mayor on Tuesday 18th October 1932. They were on their way to the Town Hall for the ceremony of handing over the Charter of Incorporation of the Borough of Brentford and Chiswick.

The Charter Mayor, Mr James Clements JP, with his Mayoress Mrs Clements at the Charter celebrations in October 1932.

Fromow's Cottage in about 1890. William Fromow established his nursery at the junction of Wellesley Road and Sutton Lane in 1828. The land was sold for building in 1932 when Beverley, Belgrave and Beaumont Courts were built on the site. Fromow's Nurseries continued on a site in Acton Lane near Chiswick Park Station until 1970.

Sutton Lane about 1900. The Alms Houses on the left were built about 1700 and were demolished in 1957, when Sutton Close flats were built on the site. This scene now fronts onto the busy A4.

Sutton Lane in the early 1920s showing the Queen's Head Public House before it was rebuilt in 1925, and the Lecture Hall which went out of use in the late 1930s and is now a gymnasium.

An early view, before the First World War, of the south west corner of Turnham Green at the junction of Heathfield Gardens and Sutton Lane. The lack of traffic, compared with today, is very noticeable. Imagine posing for a picture on that corner now!

A First World War tank displayed on the north west corner of the Green. This was given to the people of Chiswick in 1920 in recognition of the money they had raised for the war effort during the First War. It stood there until it was cut up for scrap metal in May 1937.

A panorama of the High Road, the oldest known photograph of Turnham Green, taken on the evening of 16th August 1863. In the centre can be seen the Crown and Anchor, a public house from the 1830s, the single story building to the left is the smithy. A pump, providing water for

many purposes, can be seen on the north side of the Green. The area appears deserted because moving figures were lost in the long exposure time needed to take the photograph. The duck pond on the east corner of the Green can be seen on the right.

North side of the High Road about 1910, showing the shops which were shortly to be demolished to make way for the Chiswick Empire.

Barratt's the undertakers being demolished in 1911. According to the lettering over the fascia the firm had been established since 1781. Bisley's printing works and Barratts premises were both rebuilt on approximately the same sites.

Chiswick Empire, opened by Sir Oswald Stoll in 1912 in spite of considerable local opposition to having a music hall in the area. Starting as a music hall it was later used for many different forms of entertainment. It closed in June 1959, with the pianist Liberace giving a virtuoso performance on the last night, and was replaced by the office block called Empire House in 1961. On the back of this postcard is written 'this is a picture of the London Music Hall which was burnt down.' It was not exactly burnt down but the serious fire of August 1913 did cause the Empire to close for three months.

Essex Place, behind the High Road, looking west, in the 1920s. The side view of the Chiswick Empire may be seen at the end of the passage. The street is still gas lit.

Primrose Day in April 1926. Mrs Grant Morden, wife of the MP for Brentford and Chiswick, selling primroses in aid of the Chiswick Philanthropic Society's appeal for the needy old folk.

Horse bus, taken in the 1880s. The London General Omnibus Company had stabling for some of their horses in Stamford Brook Road from 1877 to 1909.

The Old Pack Horse on the corner of Acton Lane and the High Road in the 1890s. It had been a public house since the middle of the seventeenth century although the building was probably older than that.

The High Road looking east in about 1915, showing the Empire and the Old Pack Horse, rebuilt in 1911.

The High Road and the north west corner of the Green before 1911 when the buildings on the left of the picture were demolished. The very prominent sign advertises the Old Pack Horse Public House on the opposite side of the road.

The corner of the High Road and Acton Lane before the First World War showing the Old Pack Horse with a new front, taken about 1905. The sign proudly describing the trains to London directs passengers round the corner to Chiswick Park and Acton Green Station (see next page).

Chiswick Park Station, a view of 1906 when it was known as Chiswick Park and Acton Green Station. It took its present name in 1910 and was rebuilt in 1931-2.

The Royal Standard Laundry in Bollo Lane, one of several laundries in the area, many of which had receiving offices in the High Road. It flourished from the beginning of the century until the 1970s. The Royal Standard's receiving office was at 402 High Road.

Henry Foley, picture framer, photographed in 1908. The basement of his shop at Number 468 High Road was the first headquarters of the 1st West London Scout Troop (also known as the 1st Chiswick) one of the earliest scout troops, formed in 1908. The scout master Tom Foley was the son of the proprietor.

The Grange, a 'gothic' building, was built about 1874 by William Trehearne, Surveyor to the Chiswick Improvement Commissioners. (He is seen with the Commissioners on page 22.) It stood on the south side of the High Road near Gunnersbury Station. It was later occupied by Alfred Kendall, the builder who developed Grange Road in the 1890s.

The interior of the Grange, from a sale catalogue of 1889. The house was demolished in the late 1930s and a block of flats with the same name built on the site in 1939.

Gunnersbury High School for Girls, about 1904, next to The Grange. The School flourished from about 1894 to 1916. The site is now occupied by a block of flats.

Gunnersbury Station before the First World War. It was opened in 1869, being called Brentford Road until 1871 and was redeveloped when the IBM office block was built in 1965.

A Metropolitan District train from Richmond to New Cross entering Gunnersbury Station, about 1901/02.

The London General Omnibus Company opened its central works for the overhaul of its buses in 1921-22 opposite Gunnersbury Station. At its peak it was one of the largest employers in the area. The works were closed in 1988 and the site is scheduled to be redeveloped as a Business Park.

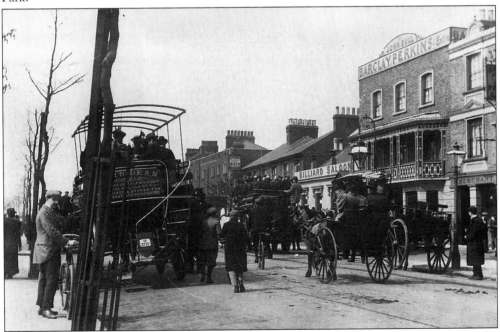

Holiday makers preparing for a day in the country outside the John Bull Public House on the north side of the High Road opposite Gunnersbury Station in 1895.

Jeffrey's Market Garden at the turn of the century. Established by 1826 at the corner of Gunnersbury Lane and the High Road it was in operation until the coming of the Great West Road in the 1920s.

Chiswick Roundabout being built at the junction of the Great West Road with Chiswick High Road in 1957. Most of Clarence Road and Surrey Crescent are now lost and also the public houses the Crown (seen in the centre of the photograph) and the Gardeners Arms (on the extreme right). This is now one of the busiest roundabouts in London.

Opposite: The High Road in the 1920s looking eastwards from a spot between Clarence Road and Surrey Crescent towards the area that was to become the Chiswick Roundabout. In the centre is the Gardeners Arms Public House. St James Church, demolished in 1989, can be seen in the distance.

The Chiswick Flyover in 1964. Part of the original flyover can be seen in the centre with one of the new piers supporting the elevated section of the motorway being built along the line of the Great West Road.

First published 1994
Reprinted 1994
Copyright © Carolyn and Peter Hammond, 1994

The Chalford Publishing Company Limited
St Mary's Mill, Chalford, Stroud
Gloucestershire GL6 8NX

ISBN 0 7524 0001 0

Typesetting and origination by
Alan Sutton Limited
Printed in Great Britain by
Redwood Books, Trowbridge